A Certain Ache:

Poems in Women's Voices

by

Bonnie Wehle

Finishing Line Press
Georgetown, Kentucky

A Certain Ache:

Poems in Women's Voices

Copyright © 2022 by Bonnie Wehle
ISBN 978-1-64662-870-4 First Edition
All rights reserved under International and Pan-American Copyright Conventions. No part of this book may be reproduced in any manner whatsoever without written permission from the publisher, except in the case of brief quotations embodied in critical articles and reviews.

ACKNOWLEDGMENTS

I am grateful to the editors of the following publications in which some of these works first appeared, sometimes in a slightly different form:

Frida! appeared in *Metaforologia Gaceta Literaria* (2018)
Artemisia Tells the Truth appeared as Artemisia in *Valley Voices* (2019)
Eve Writes to Her Great-granddaughters appeared as To My Great-granddaughters *in HerWords: A Quarterly Literary Magazine for Women/* Black Mountain Press (2020)
The Magician's Wife appeared in *Red Rock Review* (2019)

A special thanks to the teachers, mentors, fellow poets, friends and relatives who have taught, encouraged, supported, and believed in me. You have my deepest gratitude.

Publisher: Leah Huete de Maines
Editor: Christen Kincaid
Cover Art: Bonnie Wehle
Author Photo: Ana C. Blum
Cover Design: Elizabeth Maines McCleavy

Order online: www.finishinglinepress.com
        also available on amazon.com

Author inquiries and mail orders:
Finishing Line Press
PO Box 1626
Georgetown, Kentucky 40324
USA

Table of Contents

Frida: After the Farewell Party, She Paints a Portrait the Client Hates 1

Frida! 3

Artemisia Tells the Truth 5

Maria Gertrudis Barceló, 1805-1852 6

Eve Writes to Her Great-granddaughters 8

Käthe 9

Agnes, Before They Lock the Doors for the Day 11

Suzette: The Magician's Wife 12

Hedy, After Her Arrest for Shoplifting 13

Marie: The Parisian Defines Feminine for Picasso 14

Madame C.: X-rayed 15

Mileva: Excerpts from Her Book of Questions 16

Sophie Takes Inventory 17

Twyla, After Her Husband of Thirty Years Asks for a Divorce 18

Charlotte 19

Carrie: The Air She Breathes 20

Gloria, Having Put Her Paints Away 21

Beth: Flying Home 22

Amelia: Final Entries 23

Notes 25

*Dedicated to women throughout time
who spoke but were not heard;
who raised their voices
even when no one was listening.*

*There's really no such thing as the 'voiceless'.
There are only the deliberately silenced,
or the preferably unheard.
Arundhati Roy*

Frida: After the Farewell Party, She Paints a Portrait the Client Hates

I
Let me remind you how it started:

All the beautiful people were there—
artists, writers, financiers, politicians.
Dorothy wanted to say good-bye.
Planning a trip, she said.

Champagne in Baccarat, patés on Wedgewood,
left over from better times,
tiny cakes on sterling platters, slightly tarnished.
Great party...the perfect hostess, everyone agreed.

A young widow, an aspiring actress with few scenes—
rich lovers, a fleeing fiancé,
and at least a decade of therapy.
Very little talent and no luck, someone whispered.

Apparel purchased with pawned diamonds,
a lavish lifestyle without the funds—
the one part she acted well,
Needs to find a rich husband, another scoffed.

Bon voyages wished, shoulders hugged, cheeks kissed,
no one bothered to ask her destination.
For four hours, just inside the balcony of her tenth floor flat,
she composed the notes—*Farewell, Farewell*, she wrote.

By then the cigarette pack was empty, the vodka was gone.
They found her on the sidewalk still
in her black velvet gown and corsage of yellow roses.

II

Now the painting, you tell me, is not what you wanted—
you wanted to destroy it with a pair of library scissors,
it is not a portrait, you say.
True, it is not just a head and shoulders.

Her whole body, over the balcony,
in the air, on the sidewalk,
bloody, dead.
No wings, *alas*, to fly.

For her, I cannot paint what is not—
I cannot paint fantasy.
For her, it must be truth—
and how is the truth not a portrait?

Doesn't her ending define her, after all?
The leap that turns life to death,
alive to dead—
isn't that everyone's final portrait?

But, yes, I will rub out the words.
No one will know it was you who ordered
such a gruesome thing.

Frida!

How I relish the market's music of babble and laughter,
its perfume of calla lilies, spices, freshly baked bread.
I load my basket with *calabacitas*,
tomatoes, avocados, *nopalitos*,
corn tortillas, *queso fresco*—
ingredients for our lunch,
and—to paint—a small melon.

I stop at the confectioner's stall—chocolate
mixed with cinnamon and crushed almonds—
my favorite.
Plain chocolate is not enough.
I select some pieces, broken,
like my body, my heart.
All that's whole is my love for Diego.
What he returns is not enough.

***

Cluttering my shelves—
the babies I can't have.
Dolls—cheap, pricey, papier mâché, Chinese,
two from Paris, old fashioned,
their loose heads tilting to one side.
Between two rag dolls, a human fetus
in a jar of formaldehyde—
don't ask from where.
On the table, a tiny house stuffed with tiny furniture,
the empty crib of my barrenness beside my bed.

So many losses,
Diego doesn't come anymore.
Basta. Enough, I say.
I fill my heart's void with monkeys, dogs, parrots,
paint images of fetuses,

and myself, so often myself—and blood.
You may call me a surrealist, like Señor Dali,
but I always paint the truth—my truth—
though *I would like to see lions come out of that bookshelf
and not books.*

***

To me, there is little difference between love
and art, between passion and madness.
Madness is yellow, I am sure of that.
Van Gogh's house in Arles, yellow.
Mine, blue, deep and intense.
For sadness?
No, for purity.

But black—black
is for nothing—and everything.
Black is for holes, empty wombs,
black borders, black moods.
Black inkblots, the menstrual blood
that each month reminds me of my unborn babies.

In my sketchbook,
so much is outlined in black—
caged—
by love and suffering,
so much suffering.
All those self-portraits—
all those disembodied legs and feet I draw
to sever the hurt. Canvases can't
        feel the pain.

Artemisia Tells the Truth
    (Artemisia Gentileschi 1593–c. 1656)

Don't tell me I can't cry rape or testify in court. I will.
It is true, it is true, it is true.

    Anxious Susanna bathes in a stone pool. Watched
    by leering faces, she pulls her gown around her naked body.

And don't tell me a woman can't be an artist,
I paint better than the lot of you.

    folds of cloth contrast with the smoothness of her skin,
    as she leans away from the lecherous grins.

True, I paint women as victims or victors, over and over.
For us there is little in between.

Yes, I am that Susanna, the maiden at whom the elders ogle.
I am also Judith, the warrior, who slays the evil Holofernes.

    Brightly lit arms come together in struggle and strength,
    his face horror ridden, hers set in resolve.

I have *the spirit of Caesar in the soul of a woman.*
I will show what a woman can do.

    The bloody sword severs his head.
    His life fluid soaks the sheet red.

You male artists may lord your talent over me,
feign acceptance, but I am one of you more than you know.

Ignore me if you wish, my paintings will hang
above your coffins.

Maria Gertrudis Barceló
1805–1852

> *"[Madame La Tules is] a stately dame of a certain age, the possessor of a portion of that shrewd sense and fascinating manner necessary to allure the wayward, inexperienced youth to the hall of final ruin."*
> Susan Shelby Magoffin, Santa Fe, New Mexico, 1846

I sit on the mound of her grave,
its headstone, my backrest.
Above me a raven settles on a branch.
A black feather flutters to the grass. The breeze
quakes the aspen leaves into a soft chatter.
Though I am not cold, I shiver.

    Luring youth to final ruin, Ha!
    En vida, I was known as, La Tules, short for Gertrudis.
    Many thought me charming, lovely, shrewd, and brilliant,
    but those homely old hags, jealous of my beauty.

The raven croaks and shifts restlessly.

    Some even called me the Queen of Sin.
    And that *mujer horrible* wrote such evil things about me.
    I was not a sinner, no, *pero es verdad*,
    I was the best Monte player in all of New Mexico.

The bird flaps his wings, moves to a lower branch to scan for prey.

    And I ran the finest casino in Santa Fe.
    Los hombres drank my liquor, gambled at my tables,
    then called me names when they lost.
    Ha! I think they were secretly in love with me.

The raven drops to the ground, returns to the tree with an insect in his beak.

        Why do people so hate the success of others?
        I adopted orphan girls, gave *mucho*
        dinero to the poor *y la Iglesia*.
        yet some of those bastards' words were truly cruel.

From deep in the aspen, the bird mutters guttural sounds I've not heard before.

        ¡Ay!, and their stories were believed,
        passed down as truth.
        In some places *nosotros los méxicanos*
        are still being called immoral, or worse. *¡Qué triste!*

The wind quickens.
The raven rises, a fury of feathers.
A shadow, too big to be his, passes over me.

Eve Writes to Her Great-granddaughters

I want to write to you of summer peaches,
plums fresh off the branch,
their lusciousness in my mouth.

Instead, I gnaw
on fruit from an apple tree in a garden
someone else once wrote about,

trying to persuade me it was my own fault,
the pestilence, pain, fighting, smiting.
The shame.

Trying to tell me how perfect it all was,
the purring panthers, curly-coated ungulates,
winged things of all sizes

and every sort of blooming vine,
until an asp slithered down and seduced me with lies.
Until angels, with clumsy wings, convinced me

I could fly, then let me fall,
and failed to tell me there were still snakes in the trees,
their tongues flicking with deceit.

And there they remain, my darlings.
Don't be fooled,
you will find only their sloughed skin by the roadside.

Käthe

> *"It is right for us to weep for our loved ones, but we must be worthy heirs."*
> Käthe Kollwitz, 1867–1945

Germany, 1916.

Where have my children gone?
I long to have them back,
to dance with them in springtime
when Peter came with tulips.

All of Germany is mourning.
My mother refuses to give in to grief.
I am not so stubborn.
My work takes me back to it again and again.

There is too much sorrow.
When I pick up charcoal to draw,
to crush the sadness out,
vent my angry passion on paper,

the burnt parts of my soul feel kinship
with the wood become carbon,
black lines, some rubbed into smudges.
Even the gray is dark.

Lines, lines are my strength and my weakness.
Lines tell the tales.
Sometimes they shout so loud
I have to cover my eyes.

My hands draw anguished faces.
I weep along with them,
but feel no relief.
I cannot separate my heart from my work.

I make sketches, a hundred, of death,
use my darkest sticks,
thick strong lines.
Still the sorrow stings.

Agnes, Before They Lock the Doors for the Day

How often I sit
and watch the gulls dance over the water
as the waning day casts its colors on the lake,
talk back to the calling loons,
wish on the first evening star.

And think of mother
brushing my hair in her long measured stokes,
and father, who brought me books and baubles,
dried my tears on his carefully folded white handkerchief.
They hoped for me a life, long-lived, children to name after them,
a garden with roses.

Instead I paint fevered pictures, so many in my mind,
covered in thick black scrawls,
sign them AGNES in bold letters,
wear mother's paisley shawl to cover my shoulders,
never speak of the dreams,
shattered, the windows, broken,
the hard edges that won't soften.

Suzette: The Magician's Wife

All those years he pulled rabbits out of hats for me,
waved his wand over my days,
before he made himself disappear,
dropped the world he had conjured
outside my door,
        let it shatter on the sidewalk.

I took down the oiled canvases I had made
in that abracadabra life,
turned their bright faces to the walls,
replanted the garden with bluebells,
bought new bed linens
        in a deep shade of red.

The only rabbits these days are the wild ones
that hide under my hedge.
Each evening I watch them creep out,
with a courage
        I'm not sure I have.

On the stark white walls,
I hang somber tones, dark colors.
Imaginings trapped deep inside
leap from the frames,
hooded figures grab outward,
or flee backward into the scene.
No rabbits,
        just their holes.

I color my hair with purple streaks,
wear aqua and gold,
wildly patterned socks,
outline my mouth in pink,
my eyes in black kohl.
My mirror image—
        a self-portrait I can no longer paint.

Hedy, After Her Arrest for Shoplifting

I tell you beauty is a curse
and for that I will probably be cursed
by those who wish for it.
Be careful, is my advice.

The worship of audiences intoxicates, yes,
but in pre-war Austria applause
was the thunder of a threatening storm.
Accolades are for roles acted out
in refuge behind masks of others' making.

Nothing about me is real, not even my name.
I am a paper doll. Cutout clothes hang
from my shoulders by little tabs—
the fragility of fame
ready to break with the slightest tug.

Science is my true love,
my brain bristles with ideas, inventions.
Women aren't welcome in that field,
a painful lesson I learned.

> *Sorry Miss Lamarr,*
> *we can't use your torpedo guidance system*
> *because our boys wouldn't feel safe using a device*
> *invented by a woman. Now be a good girl*
> *and use that pretty face of yours to sell war bonds.*

Damn you beauty, I want my soul back.

Marie: The Parisian Defines Feminine for Picasso

I feel perfectly at ease with everything that is feminine.
Marie Laurencin, 1883–1956

True, I don't paint like a man.
My brushes kiss the canvas
differently from a man's. I
kiss you differently,

a gentler stroke of the tongue.
Poets and lovers, I embrace, bed, paint,
but my palette is always tender.
A certain ache draws my hand forward,

pulls my pen into lines,
my brush into blushing tints.
Lithe figures float on my paper,
dance to my bristles, inhabit my hues.

Rose-colored wraps, lavender skirts,
pale sleeves on white shoulders,
pink flowers woven into copious curls,
these are my loves, *mes amours*.

I'll not be persuaded by the praise of men,
nor defined by their labels. I
am a woman. I paint like a woman,
pastels, silk scarves, arabesques.

Madame C.: X-rayed

Is it that I am a scientist or a woman that bothers you?
You are quick to celebrate me, praise me,

reward me, as long as you think I am without desire,
a scientist, not a human female.

After Pierre's death I thought I would never laugh again,
All I had left was my science.

Now I find I have passion
for something besides radium and polonium.

Paul, my assistant, married, yes, that's unfortunate,
but how can I not revel in such unexpected joy?

You rage, call me seductress when I show a woman's hunger.
How dare you?

Monsieur Nobel is ready to give me another prize.
The world glories in my accomplishments.

Yet you, you want me pure like the elements I discover.
I am not, so you scorn me.

Ah, but you will ignore my sins
when you need my discoveries to save you.

Mileva: Excerpts from Her Book of Questions

What else for a girl crippled from birth?
Science, my dream,
my father's dream for me.
You might as well pursue it, he said.
Women are supposed to marry, have a family,
yet who would marry me with this limp?

Albert, dear Albert.
If I hadn't bested him in math,
hadn't let him eclipse my contributions,
if I hadn't been made of glass,
if I had voiced the screech of my spirit
with the intensity of a violin,
would he have stayed?

Was it the quotidian chores he abhorred
or the gravity of me?
The *How was your day*,
his answer, mine,
the forces of attraction, the distortion of spacetime,
our laundry on the line, the dirt on our faces?

Who matters,
those who change the course of knowledge
or those who love them,
those who speak loudly,
or the quiet casualties?

Sophie Takes Inventory

I'm not sure why I keep
all those books, far too many of them
lining the shelves in the living room,
punctuated every now and then
by pieces of depression glass.
Depressing glass, I call it.

In my husband's closet, his suits, arranged by color,
two black, two blue, three gray,
still balance on their wooden hangers,
a triangle of white handkerchief
peeking from the pocket of each.
His ties, 28 of them, drape the end wall,
except the one he hung himself with 33 years ago.

All that money I spent on therapy—
I still have the receipts—
and my daughter, who brings my meals each evening,
steals from me, twenty-dollar bills keep going missing.
I know how many I had.
My son feigns a hunt for them, lifting the doilies on tables,
the corners of the rugs in every room.
He's not fooling me.

The hospice nurse who comes on Thursdays, I am sure,
poisons the tea she serves in the bone china cups
I inherited from my mother.
The bitter taste gives it away.

Twyla, After Her Husband of Thirty Years Asks for a Divorce

In the basement corner,
the rusty two-wheeler from my ninth birthday leans
against Dad's work bench.
His tools hang on the pegboard rack over their painted shapes,
guidance for those who tend not to put them back in their place,
the adjustable wrench still missing.

My brother, just two years older than me,
took his life last June,
left his dog at the shelter for me to reclaim.
Uncle Jack died three years before,
my father the next spring.

I haven't lived here since high school,
since those cartwheels on the summer grass,
wrestling matches with my brother,
fishing on the lake.
A dollar for the first bass, two for the most.

In the attic, ornaments from all our Christmases,
tinsels of remembrance stashed with my dolls,
my brother's toy trucks, Aunt Jane's wedding dress.
The same dishrag plugs the knothole on the back wall.

Bats, attic companions I have never warmed to,
fly downstairs on warm nights.
I tie a scarf around my head,
half-believing the myth they will tangle in my in hair,
close them in the bathroom,
tuck a towel under the door, sleep on the sofa.

I should be clearing out the house.
I come on weekends,
huddle in an armchair.
I know I need to let go
like the flaking paint on the siding,
the loose shingles on the roof.

Charlotte

The fellow behind the bar tells me of the suicides,
the ghost in room 242, of the old man
who fixed things with butter knives—
the maids still find them now and then.
Phantom children play in the hall,
where guests sometimes hear a ball bouncing.

He has tales, for sure, but I feel comfortable
here in the lounge of this old hotel,
wearing the lace dress I got
from the Better Days Thrift Store,
drinking Seven and Seven,
tall glass, lots of ice.
Who orders that anymore?

Vintage. Like me.
I belong here, yes,
more than other places I have stayed.
Ghosts, I can handle, I've carried some around for years.
But why, I wonder, had the suicides
chosen to do it here.
It seems like a good place to live.
Maybe it's a good place to die.

Carrie: The Air She Breathes

The stench of cleanliness,
bottled bleach, bottled grief,
the scent of my childhood,
my years coming to womanhood.

Identical covers bed after bed, white,
the color of clean, everything clean
except the air into which she coughed
from lungs that wouldn't heal.

My Sundays of mourning,
visits to her in the hospital,
the comforting touch of her skin
I had waited all week to feel,

fragile mother and daughter time
edged with an acrid odor
so unlike the sleepy fragrance
in my bed this Sunday morning.

Gloria, Having Put Her Paints Away

Please don't open that door, dear.
Stacked neatly inside, boxes and boxes,
beautiful round hat boxes covered in floral paper
packed with memories that sting
(I prefer not to call them regrets)

enticements that once seemed worthy—
crispy corsages, love notes, one or two engagement rings,
reminders of sins best forgotten,
friends abandoned, trusts betrayed.
And paintings, lots of paintings stacked against the wall.

That's what artists do, darling,
they put onto canvas the burdens
they can't keep lugging around.
I have made dozens of paintings of my life,
pictures and pictures to get out of my head.

I try not to open the closet,
though drawn there like a perverse lover.
Will I ever be able to lock that door,
be faced only with my own face in the mirror,
the sadness I camouflage with jars and jars of concealer?

Have I been successful?
Tell me you can't see it, dear.
It wants always to bolt out
like my son launching
off the balcony before my eyes.

Did I ever paint his picture,
that terrace I live with every day,
the regret at my inability to stop him?
Keep painting, Gloria.
More pictures, more pictures.

Beth: Flying Home

I climb into the cockpit, clutching my basket to my breast,
the orange and purple one given me in Ghana.
Tucked beneath my clothes,
beads I strung with the tiny San women of Botswana,
their fears and fights when the government wanted their land
for the diamonds it hid,
snipers I dodged on the landing strip in Mali,
children taken to Kenya for medical care,
they are all in there, tightly packed.

> She sits in her comfortable chair, an old recliner
> that doesn't fit her anything like a pilot's seat,
> pulls her well-worn flight jacket
> tightly around her shoulders.

I go through the Cessna's pre-takeoff check,
a list of things I know by heart,
double my silk scarf loosely around my neck,
and shove the basket deep beneath my seat.
I lower the flaps, push in the throttle,
pull back on the joystick and I'm aloft,
climbing above the vast Kalahari,
above cumulonimbi of my life,
Africa below me.

> She rubs her arthritic hands,
> the ones that threaded the beads,
> guided the plane, packed the basket.
> Africa inside her.

Amelia: Final Entries

> *Please don't be concerned. It just seems that I must try this flight.*
> Amelia Earhart to husband George Palmer (G.P.) Putnam

Aviator's Log—1937
Uninhabited Island in Central Pacific

July 4
Two days since crash.
Fred badly hurt.
Can't figure how we missed Howland,
why radio messages haven't gotten through.
why no responses to pleas for help.

July 5
Still transmitting, but no answers.
Managing to subsist on snacks from plane,
scavenged plants, fish left by the tide,
and coconuts, if I can beat the crabs to them.
Fresh water is a problem.

July 6
Had that dream again last night.
Huge crabs all over this island after me.
I can't decide whether to keep running or to try to swim to safety.
Those monstrous beasts eat everything that ends up on the beach.

I've always tried to be realistic about the possibility
of perishing on one of my adventures.
Still, I've never really expected to. One doesn't, does one?
Or did I just insist on optimism as my best hope
and the best face to present to the world?

One last attempt to prove women
are every bit as capable as men.
Should have listened to GP.
How I used to fuss at him for calling me Freckles.
Oh, to hear him call me that again.
Dear man. Will he ever know what became of me?

July 7
I once wrote of *the focused horror of death's approach*.
Now I'm living through it.

Too much time to reflect.
Worst part of this slow process.
Bad judgement, mistakes,
so many got me here.

Can't hold on much longer.
Crabs, horrid creatures,
will pick bones
clean,
   devour   me.

One last
  because
must.

Notes

Frida, After the Farewell Party, She Paints a Portrait the Client Hates

The subject of the first part of this poem is Dorothy Donovan Hale (1905-1938), a New York socialite and aspiring actress. After her husband's death, which left her in debt, she had several unsuccessful relationships and eventually was reduced to relying on her wealthy friends, such as Claire Booth Luce, for support. On October 21, 1938, she committed suicide by jumping from her apartment balcony.

Luce commissioned Kahlo to paint Dorothy's portrait as a gift for her mother, but was appalled by the gruesomeness of the painting and gave it away to a friend. The legend on the painting read: "In the city of New York on the 21st of the month of October 1938, at six in the morning, Mrs. DOROTHY HALE committed suicide by throwing herself out of a window of the Hampshire House building. In her memory, [The Suicide of Dorothy Hale...painted at the request of Clare Boothe Luce, for the mother of Dorothy] this retablo, having executed it FRIDA KAHLO.

The painting can be seen on various online sites.

Frida!

Frida Kahlo was born on July 6, 1907, but she claimed to have been born in 1910, since that was the year of the outbreak of the Mexican Revolution. She was disabled by polio as a child, and at age eighteen, was badly hurt in a bus accident. Her injury caused her lifelong pain and medical problems, including the inability to have children. She met Diego Rivera through her interest in the Mexican Communist party. They were married in 1929. It was a tumultuous marriage that ended in divorce in 1939. They remarried in 1940.

Stylistically, Frida drew on the Mexican folk art tradition, although she was at times labeled a surrealist. As her suffering from her injury worsened, she underwent several operations and numerous hospitalizations. She died in 1954.

The English phrase in italics is a quote in translation.

Artemisia Tells the Truth

Artemisia Gentileschi (1593–1652) was an Italian Baroque painter, and one of the most celebrated female artists of the 17th century. When she was 17, she was raped by a family friend, the artist Agostino Tassi. Her father took him to court and Artemisia testified at the trial, which was unusual at the time. Tassi was found guilty and banished from Rome, but the punishment was never enforced. After her marriage to a little-known Florentine artist, Gentileschi continued her career in Florence, where she associated with some of the most important artists, writers and thinkers of the time, although she had to fight for fair compensation and validity. She also ran a successful art school in Naples for 25 years, traveled and lived throughout Europe and England, and gained the patronage of royalty, including Charles I.

Two of Artemisia's most famous works, of which she painted several versions, are referenced in this poem: "Susanna and the Elders," (the first version painted in 1610, others between 1622 and 1630) and "Judith and Holofernes,"(the first one done in 1611, others between 1612 and 1620). These paintings can be seen on several online sites.

The phrases in italics are her own words.

Maria Gertrudis Barceló, 1805–1852

Doña Gertrudis Barceló, also known as Doña Tules and "The Queen of Sin," lived in Santa Fe in the mid 19th century, at the time New Mexico became part of the United States. Mexicans such as Doña Tules, who automatically became American citizens, were looked down upon by the white Americans. But Doña Tules became a prominent businesswoman and casino operator and was skilled in dealing a game known as Monte. She became very wealthy and controversial, but was extremely generous, giving money and gifts to the Catholic Church and needy families, and adopting two children.

Käthe

Käthe Schmidt Kollwitz was born in 1867 in East Prussia. In 1891, she married Dr. Karl Kollwitz, a medical doctor, who practiced in Berlin. They had two sons. Peter, the younger one, was killed in WWI.

Kollwitz was primarily a graphic artist relying on line rather than color. She is known for her drawings (pencil and charcoal) and prints (woodcuts, etchings and lithographs) focusing on social issues. Having lived through two world wars in which her country was deeply involved, death and sorrow played a large role in her work.

Photos of her death series pieces can be viewed at
https://www.kollwitz.de/en/series-death-overview

Hedy, After Her Arrest for Shoplifting

Hedy Lamarr was born Hedwig Eva Maria Kiesler in Austria in 1914. She met with considerable success as a stage actress in Austria. At 18, she married a 33 year-old Viennese arms merchant, but finding it unbearable after several years, she fled to Paris.

She was subsequently discovered by Louis B. Mayer, who promoted her in Hollywood as "the world's most beautiful woman." She played opposite some of Hollywood's major leading men, often cast as the exotic seductress. She was married and divorced six times and was plagued by drugs and alcohol.

Having a lifelong interest in science, Lamarr enjoyed inventing things. Together with composer and pianist George Antheil, she invented and patented a torpedo guidance system based on frequency hopping. The system, used in Bluetooth technology today, was turned down by the Navy. Instead they asked her sell war bonds. In her later years, she was twice arrested for shoplifting, though never indicted. She died in 2000.

Marie: The Parisian Defines Feminine for Picasso

Marie Laurencin was a French painter, a contemporary of Picasso, Braque and Matisse, with whom she was closely associated. For many years she was the lover of the poet Guillaume Apollinaire, and a friend of Gertrude Stein and Alice B. Toklas. In her later career she focused mainly on portraits of women. Her work hangs in art museums throughout the U.S., Japan and Europe, including the *Musée de l'Orangerie* in Paris, the Museum of Modern Art in New York, the Tate Gallery in London, and the Hermitage Museum in St. Petersburg.

Her work can be seen on various online sites.

Madame C.: X-rayed

Marie Skłodowska Curie was born in 1867 in Warsaw, Poland. When she was 24 she went to Paris to continue her education in science. She married Pierre Curie in 1895. They worked together and in 1903 shared a Nobel Prize in physics. Pierre was killed in a road accident in 1906 and Marie carried on by herself. She developed the theory of radioactivity (a term she coined) and discovered the elements polonium and radium. In 1911, she won a second Nobel Prize, this one in chemistry. She was the first woman to win a Nobel Prize and the first person and only woman to win the Prizes in two different fields. Just prior to winning the second Prize, her affair with her married assistant, Paul Langevin, became a public scandal.

She established the Radium Institute of the University of Paris, which under her guidance produced four more Nobel winners. She received numerous other awards and honors before she died at age 66 from long-term exposure to radiation.

Mileva: Excerpts from Her Book of Questions

Mileva Marić Einstein, was born in Serbia in 1875 with a deformed hip and leg. Having an interest and aptitude in science, at age 21 she entered the Zurich Polytechnic, in Zurich, Switzerland, the only female in the class. Here she met Albert Einstein, who wooed her by joining in the concerts Mileva and the other women in her pension held each evening. Albert played the violin.

After their marriage in 1903, Albert, failing to find an academic position went to work in a patent office. During this time he began formulating some of his early theories. It is said that Mileva helped him with some of these theories and equations, though her name never appeared on any of the published papers.

After their divorce in 1919, Einstein gave up his two sons and married his cousin. Though seriously ill much of the time, Mileva raised the boys on her own. She died alone in a hospital on August 4, 1948 repeating the single word "no." She was 73.

Gloria, Having Put Her Paints Away

Gloria Vanderbilt (1924-2019) inherited great wealth at an early age, but her young years were filled with instability and uncertainty. As an adult she had four marriages and countless affairs with prominent men.

In addition to having been a fashion icon, socialite and writer of numerous books, Gloria became known for her art—oil painting, watercolors and pastels—with several one-woman shows. She also created designs for linen, pottery and glassware. Carter Cooper, the oldest son from her third marriage, jumped from the family's 14th-floor balcony at age 23.

Her art can be seen on several online sites including, http://www.artnet.com/artists/gloria-vanderbilt/

Amelia: Final Entries

This poem was based on the premise that having missed her intended landing site of Howland Island, Amelia Earhart crash landed about 400 miles southeast, on Gardiner Island, now called Nikumaroro. While there are records of radio broadcasts from her that appear to have originated from Gardiner, as well as archeological evidence of her presence on the island, there is also substantial witness testimony of her presence on Saipan. In the latter scenario she is thought to have landed on one of the Marshall Islands, been picked up by the Japanese, and taken to Saipan where she was held prisoner and died of unknown causes, possibly execution as a spy.

The italicized phrase is quoted from Traci Brimhall's essay, "Archival Voyeur: Searching for Secrets in Amelia Earhart's Lost Poems," in *New England Review*, Vol 40, No. 4 (2019). (Shared on LitHub.)

Bonnie Wehle was born in Rochester, New York and raised in both Rochester and Tucson, Arizona. She is a graduate of Wellesley College (B.A.) and the University of Oregon (M.S.). She worked for many years as an architectural historian for the California Department of Transportation and as a private consultant in historic preservation. She has made her home in several states including New York, Illinois, Oregon, California, Utah and Arizona. She presently lives in Tucson with her dog, Tillie.

Bonnie took up poetry seriously after she retired. She has enjoyed going to workshops in both the U.S. and Mexico, as well as taking classes and workshops online and at the UA Poetry Center in Tucson where has served as a docent. In that capacity, she has led a monthly poetry circle in conjunction with the Pima County Library. Bonnie's work has been published in *Heron Tree Literary Journal, River Heron Review, HerWords/Black Mountain Press, Valley Voices, Red Rock Review, Sky Islands Journal, Metaforología Gaceta Literaria*, and elsewhere. Among her favorite poets are Laure-Anne Bosselaar, Linda Pastan, Marjorie Saiser, Ada Limón, and Li Young Lee. Some of her favorite poems are "Ithaca" by Constantine Cavafy, "Those Winter Sundays" by Robert Hayden, "The Peace of Wild Things" by Wendell Berry, "Garden" by Victoria Redel, and "Rooms Remembered" by Laure-Anne Bosselaar.

Website: bonniewehle.com

www.ingramcontent.com/pod-product-compliance
Lightning Source LLC
LaVergne TN
LVHW040117080426
835507LV00041B/1187